BOXFISH

Samantha Bell

Published in the United States of America by Cherry Lake Publishing
Ann Arbor, Michigan
www.cherrylakepublishing.com

Consultants: Dominique A. Didier, PhD, Associate Professor, Department of Biology, Millersville University;
Malcom S. Gordon, Professor, Department of Ecology and Evolutionary Biology, University of California Los Angeles;
Marla Conn, ReadAbility, Inc.
Book design: Sleeping Bear Press

Photo Credits: ©kaschibo/Shutterstock Images, cover, 1, 9, 21; ©DJ Mattaar/Shutterstock Images, 5; ©John Anderson/
Thinkstock, 6; ©Durden Images/Shutterstock Images, 7; ©Alexander1701/Dreamstime.com, 11; ©Michèle Tétrault/
Thinkstock, 13; ©orlandin/Shutterstock Images, 15, 17; ©Marco Lijoi/Dreamstime.com, 18; ©Karl Keller/Shutterstock
Images, 23; ©Stubblefield Photography/Shutterstock Images, 25; ©babbagecabbage/http://www.flickr.com/ CC-BY-2.0,
27; ©Lauren Williams/Dreamstime.com, 29

Library of Congress Cataloging-in-Publication Data

Bell, Samantha, author.
Boxfish / by Samantha Bell.
   pages cm. — (Exploring our oceans)
   Summary: "Discover facts about boxfish, including physical features, habitat, life cycle, food,
and threats to these ocean creatures. Photos, captions, and keywords supplement the narrative of
this informational text"—Provided by publisher.
   Audience: Age 8-12.
   Audience: Grades 4 to 6.
   Includes bibliographical references and index.
   ISBN 978-1-63188-017-9 (hardcover)—ISBN 978-1-63188-060-5 (pbk.)—ISBN 978-1-63188-103-9 (pdf)—
ISBN 978-1-63188-146-6 (ebook) 1. Boxfishes—Juvenile literature. I. Title. II. Title: Boxfish. III. Series: 21st century
skills library. Exploring our oceans.

QL638.O887B45 2015
597.64—dc23   2014005278

Cherry Lake Publishing would like to acknowledge the work of
The Partnership for 21st Century Skills. Please visit www.p21.org
for more information.

Printed in the United States of America
Corporate Graphics Inc.

ABOUT THE AUTHOR

Samantha Bell lives in South Carolina with her husband, four children, and lots of animals. She
has written and/or illustrated more than 20 books for children. She loves being outdoors and
learning about all the amazing wonders of nature.

TABLE OF CONTENTS

— CHAPTER 1 —

ALL COLORS AND SHAPES

With just one look, it's easy to see where boxfishes get their name. Each fish in this **family** has a hard outer covering with boxy "edges." With their strange bodies, it might surprise you to learn that boxfishes are good swimmers.

Scientists have named the boxfish family Ostraciidae. This group includes boxfishes, trunkfishes, and cowfishes. There are about 25 different species. They come in a variety of shapes, colors, and sizes. When looking at a boxfish head-on, its body resembles a **trapezoid**.

A trunkfish is shaped more like a triangle. The cowfish is rectangular. They can be blue, white, orange, yellow, and other colors. They have many different patterns of dots and lines.

The spotted boxfish is dark-colored, with spots that are white or yellow.

Although they don't look exactly alike, it's easy to know these fishes are related. Instead of scales, each one has a **carapace** that covers about two-thirds of its body. Only the fins, **peduncle**, and tail can bend. There are openings for the eyes, mouth, and fins and slits for the gills.

The body of the smooth trunkfish is narrow at the top and wider at the bottom, like a triangle!

Certain members of the boxfish family can grow up to 2 feet (61 cm) long!

Members of the boxfish family range in size from about 6 inches (15.2 cm) up to two feet (61 cm). The spotted boxfish of the western Pacific Ocean is among the smallest at 5 inches (13 cm). The smooth trunkfish is also small, growing to about 6 to 10 inches (15–25 cm) long. The yellow boxfish is much bigger at 18 inches (46 cm). The Caribbean trunkfish is one of the largest in this family. It can grow to 24 inches (61 cm) long.

Boxfishes don't travel far. They make their homes in shallow water near rocky and coral reefs and stay there. They also favor grassy areas, sand beds, and clear lagoons. In each of these habitats, ocean waves are constant and the water is often rough.

With their strange appearance, boxfishes, trunkfishes, and cowfishes might look like some of the most awkward fish in the sea. But their unusual design is actually just right for life among the waves.

THINK ABOUT IT

WHAT OTHER MARINE ANIMALS LIVE AMONG THE REEFS? ARE THEY TYPICALLY SMALLER ANIMALS OR LARGER ONES? WHY DO YOU THINK THIS IS?

This fish loves to make its home where the water is rough with waves.

ROUGH WATER, STRONG SWIMMER

Have you watched ocean waves crash on the beach? If so, it's easy to imagine how fish and other marine animals might get tossed around. But boxfishes stay right on course. They can swim in a straight path, no matter how much the water is churning. The fish's shape does all the work.

The corners of the boxy body form sharp-edged ridges called keels. On the cowfish, the keels go out past the body. They look like small horns on their heads. As a boxfish swims, the keels produce vortices, tiny

The keels on the yellow boxfish help it to swim straight in choppy waters.

whirlpools, in the water near them. When a wave pushes the front of the fish upward, the whirlpools automatically move upward above the keels. This pulls the back of the fish up, too. The fish stays level. If the front of the fish is pushed down, the whirlpools move downward. This pulls the back of the fish down, too. The boxfish moves straight through the water.

Many kinds of fishes have seven fins. Boxfishes have only five. These include a dorsal fin, an anal fin, two pectoral fins, and a **caudal** fin. But even with fewer fins, boxfishes are amazing swimmers. The way they use their fins allows them to hover, turn, and move quickly.

Boxfishes, trunkfishes, and cowfishes use their fins in different combinations to swim at three different **gaits**. Sometimes fins move the same way, and sometimes they move in opposite directions. At the slowest gait, the pectoral and anal fins move the fish forward. The caudal fin helps it steer. The next gait is faster. At this speed,

BODY DIAGRAM

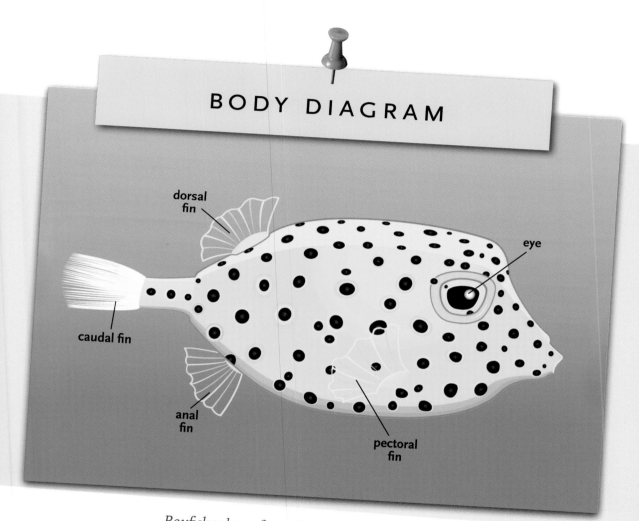

dorsal
fin

eye

caudal fin

anal
fin

pectoral
fin

Boxfishes have fewer fins than many other fish.

the fish propels itself with the pectoral, dorsal, and anal fins. To swim as fast as they can, fish use only the caudal fin. They push and then glide, push and then glide.

Boxfishes are amazing swimmers in other ways, too. Though they can't bend their bodies to turn, they do something even better. By moving their fins in a certain way, they can turn in a complete circle. This circle is so tight, it seems like they hardly move.

Boxfishes may look slow, but the design of their fins makes them very skilled swimmers.

LOOK AGAIN

AFTER STUDYING THE BODY DIAGRAM, LOOK CLOSELY AT THIS PHOTOGRAPH. CAN YOU NAME THE KINDS OF BOXFISH FINS YOU SEE IN THIS PHOTOGRAPH?

CLEVER HUNTERS

Boxfishes, trunkfishes, and cowfishes are **omnivores**. But their mouths are small, so their food must be small as well. Newly hatched fishes feed on tiny **plankton** floating in the ocean. Juvenile and adult boxfishes find their food near the reefs. They graze on the algae growing on rocks, shells, or reefs. Young and old also eat sponges and **mollusks**.

Adult members of this family eat a number of other **invertebrates**, too. Their diet includes worms, crabs, and shrimp. Some species have their favorites. The

Boxfishes find their food—such as algae, sponges, or mollusks—right where they live, in the coral reefs.

scrawled cowfish enjoys tunicates, or sea squirts.
These simple animals are found attached to rocks,
large seashells, and even the backs of crabs. Sea
anemones are another favorite food. So are sea fans.
Some adults will eat small fish.

The boxfish usually hunts and eats alone.

Some boxfish prey hide in the sand on the bottom of the ocean. Boxfishes stay close to the base of the coral reef to find them. But the fishes don't rely on their eyesight alone. Aiming their mouths at the sand, they blow small jets of water. The water pushes the sand away. The prey is uncovered and the boxfishes enjoy a good meal.

Unlike other fishes that travel in schools, boxfishes are mostly solitary swimmers. They hunt and move alone or sometimes in pairs, such as the horn-nosed boxfish. The only time they gather in large groups is during mating season.

GO DEEPER

CAN YOU THINK OF ANY OTHER MARINE ANIMALS THAT ARE OMNIVORES? DO YOU THINK THIS MAKES IT EASIER FOR THEM TO FIND FOOD? WHY OR WHY NOT?

CHAPTER 4

MATING MYSTERIES

In the boxfish family, it's easy to tell some of the males and females apart. The spotted boxfish female is brown with white spots, while the male has blue and gold spots. The female Whitley's boxfish is golden brown with white spots. The male is blue with white dots and black and white lines. However, in other species, like the yellow boxfish the male and felmale look alike.

Not much is known about the mating habits of boxfishes. Like other bony fishes, they most likely gather at certain times of the year to mate. In the tropics, these times are based on the cycles of the tide and the phases of the moon. A male may have a small number of females that he mates with at dusk. The males and females become agitated and swim around. They release their **gametes** into the water. The gametes unite by chance and become **fertilized** eggs. These eggs then float away with the currents.

It can take a baby boxfish up to a year to grow into an adult.

The eggs develop in about a week. After they hatch, the tiny larvae drift near the surface for a few more weeks. As they do, they feed on plankton. They can float along for some distance before coming to another reef.

The waves breaking against the reef below creates sound signals. The larvae pick up these signals. They start moving down toward the reef. These late-stage larvae already have the beginnings of the bony shell. They settle on the reef, hiding in the crevices of the coral.

As the larvae grow into juvenile boxfishes, they start feeding on reef animals. They may take a year or more to mature into adults. Some species change color as they grow. The juvenile yellow boxfish is bright yellow with black dots. As it gets older, the bright yellow becomes a dirty mustard color. Large adults appear bluish with yellow outlines on their plates.

Some types of boxfish change colors as they grow.

LOOK AGAIN

LOOK CLOSELY AT THIS PHOTOGRAPH. CAN YOU TELL WHAT KIND OF BOXFISH THIS IS? CAN YOU TELL IF IT IS A MALE OR FEMALE?

POISON FOR PREDATORS

Because of their small size, juvenile boxfishes are often in danger. Seabirds such as terns will snatch them up to feed to their chicks. Adult boxfishes sometimes become prey as well. But the fish's bony carapace is a strong defense. Sharks are one of the few predators that can eat them, but even then, it's often by mistake. Eating a boxfish sometimes leads to death for a shark.

Besides their shells, boxfishes have another way to protect themselves. Some juveniles have a layer of toxic **mucus** on their armor. Adult boxfishes release a highly

Why do you think boxfishes don't have many predators?

toxic poison whenever they are threatened or attacked. This poison can also be given off when they die. If a shark eats a boxfish, it swallows the poison. Boxfishes have a warning system in place, however. Their bright colors tell other animals to stay away.

Some chefs learn how to cook boxfishes so they are safe to eat. If prepared the right way, they can make a tasty meal. Boxfishes are a valuable food choice in the Caribbean. People also buy them as tourist souvenirs and decorations. When the boxfishes die, their hard shells keep the same shape. These are dried out and sold. In Southeast Asia, many people set up booths to sell dried cowfish. Even so, none of these fishes are threatened or **endangered**.

By studying boxfishes, trunkfishes, and cowfishes, we begin to understand them better. These fishes were once thought of as poor, slow-moving swimmers. People believed their hard shells were heavy and used only for protection. Now we know that their unusual shape does so much more.

When a boxfish dies, its carapace keeps its shape and color for many years. Sometimes these are sold as souvenirs!

Scientists use this information to solve other problems. Mercedes Benz used the boxfishes' shape to design a bionic car that is safe, strong, and moves through the air easily. The U.S. Navy used it to build miniature submarines that work even in rough waters. These underwater vehicles are used to find underwater mines or airplane wreckage, and for scientific research. With so many possibilities, we need to keep learning about these amazing animals.

The bright colors of the boxfish tell predators to stay away—or else!

LOOK AGAIN

LOOK CLOSELY AT THIS PHOTOGRAPH OF A BOXFISH. DO YOU THINK THE BRIGHT COLORS MAKE IT EASY PREY? WHY OR WHY NOT?

THINK ABOUT IT

- What was the most surprising fact you learned from reading this book?

- For a long time, scientists thought that boxfishes were poor swimmers. What physical features of boxfishes might cause them to think that? Based on this example, what can you conclude about our understanding of marine animals?

- Look at another book or a Web site about boxfishes. Is the information you learn different or the same as the information in this book?

- Many people think of boxfishes as colorful additions to their aquariums. But there is a risk that they might poison the other fish, especially in a smaller aquarium. If you had a saltwater aquarium, would you take that risk? Why or why not?

LEARN MORE

FURTHER READING

Allman, Toney. *From Boxfish to Aerodynamic Cars*. San Diego: Kidhaven Press, 2006.

Filisky, Michael. *Peterson First Guide to Fishes of North America*. Boston: Houghton Mifflin, 1989.

WEB SITES

Animal Diversity Web: Boxfishes
http://animaldiversity.ummz.umich.edu/accounts/Ostraciidae/pictures
This Web site has more than 10 pictures of colorful boxfishes and provides information about each.

Florida Museum of Natural History: Honeycomb Cowfish
www.flmnh.ufl.edu/fish/Gallery/Descript/honeycombCowfish
/honeycombcowfish.html
Many photos show the hexagon-shaped scale plates that give this fish the honeycomb name.

Susan Scott: Ocean Watch
www.susanscott.net/OceanWatch2010/mar-01-10.html
Learn about cowfish from marine biologist and Ocean Watch columnist Susan Scott, a Hawaii resident of 30 years.

GLOSSARY

carapace (KEHR-uh-pehss) the bony shell covering all or part of an animal

caudal (KAWD-uhl) related to the tail

endangered (en-DAYN-jurd) at risk of becoming extinct or of dying out

family (FAM-uh-lee) a group of living things that are related to each other

fertilized (FUR-tuh-lyzd) caused an egg to develop into a new organism by adding male reproductive material

gaits (GAYTS) manners or rates of movement

gametes (GA-meets) cells capable of uniting with cells of the opposite sex to form a new animal (eggs and sperm)

invertabrates (in-VER-tuh-brits) animals without a backbone

mollusks (MAH-luhsks) soft-bodied animals that have no backbones and are often enclosed in shells

mucus (MYOO-kuhs) slimy substance produced by an organism

omnivores (AHM-nuh-vorz) animals that eat both plants and other animals

peduncle (pi-DUHNG-kuhl) the narrow part of a fish's body that attaches to its tail

plankton (PLANGK-tuhn) aquatic plants and animals that are usually small and that drift in the water

trapezoid (TRAP-uh-zoid) a shape with four sides of which two are parallel

INDEX

[21ST CENTURY SKILLS LIBRARY]